HTML

Beginner's Crash Course

HTML for Beginner's Guide to Learning HTML, HTML & CSS, & Web Design

This Book Belongs To:
Matthew Blythe

not engaging in the rendering of legal, financial, medical or professional advice.

By reading this document, the reader agrees that under no circumstances are we responsible for any losses, direct or indirect, which are incurred as a result of the use of information contained within this document, including, but not limited to, errors, omissions, or inaccuracies.

Table of Contents

8

Introduction

HTML is the road that everyone needs to walk down to create the perfect webpage. Developing your own webpage and putting it online can be daunting, especially if you're as computer illiterate as I was the first time I tried. But that's OK! You can't expect to understand everything the very moment you begin building an online presence.

Don't worry if you don't always understand exactly what it is you're doing. Seriously, you don't actually need to understand everything that's happening. There's a difference between programming and coding. You're going to be programming; you won't have to create all the coded algorithms yourself, so don't be afraid. The more you explore, the more you'll understand. Hey, you might even decide to give coding a try, but that's another book for another time. Right now, all you need to know is that you're in very good hands and that you're going to be designing your own webpage. In no time at all, you'll be flying through it!

So sit back and prepare to have your brain loaded with all of the basics you'll need to really begin experimenting and doing cool things with your computer. The coming pages provide the foundation and explanations, and you'll be able to test these out with your own computer while we work through them together.

First, some background. In 1991, Sir Timothy John Berners-Lee created the first version of HyperText Markup Language, which is otherwise known as HTML. The standard version was published later, in 1995. In 1999, a major version of HTML known as HTML 4.01 was released. This is the most successful version of HTML to date. In the year 2012, HTML5 was released. HTML5 is currently the latest version and is an extension to HTML 4.01.

In this book, we will look at the important basic tags in HTML. With these, you can easily create a simple webpage of your own. All the topics are explained with examples for your better understanding.

I hope you'll like the book. Happy Reading!

Chapter 1:
HTML Editors & Elements

Editors

You can write HTML using text editors like Notepad or TextEdit, or you can use professional editors for HTML like Sublime Text or Microsoft WebMatrix. While learning HTML, it's best to use the text editors provided by your operating system, which are simpler.

By following the four simple steps given below you can create your first webpage using Notepad.

1. Open Notepad

2. Write the HTML code in notepad

3. Save the HTML page with the .html extension

4. Open the saved HTML page in your browser

HTML elements

All HTML documents are a collection of HTML elements that are written using a start tag, some content and an end tag. Everything from the start to end tags are HTML elements. Almost all the HTML elements are defined using a start tag. You must add an end tag if there is content present in the element.

Syntax:

<tagname>content</tagname>

The table below shows a few simple tags:

Start tag	Element content	End tag
<h1>	The text in between these tags will be the heading 1.	</h1>
<p>	The text within these tags will start a paragraph.	</p>
 	This tag will insert a line break.	This doesn't have an end tag.

Nested HTML elements

In HTML, elements can be placed within other elements. This is called nesting of elements, and the elements that are placed inside are called nested elements. All documents in HTML contain nested elements. Here is an example in which four nested elements are present.

Example

<!DOCTYPE html>

<html>

<body>

<h1> This text will be a heading.</h1>

<p> This will be a new paragraph.</p>

</body>

\</html>

In the above example, the tag \<html> defines the complete document. This tag ends with \</html> and contains another element \<body> which defines the body of the document. Even the \<body> tag has an end tag, \</body>.

There are also two other tags inside the end tag, \<h1> and \<p>. They end with \</h1> and \</p> respectively. Content can be placed within the tags for the desired action to be performed on them. Adding an end tag for the elements in HTML is a must for most of the tags.

Empty HTML elements

The elements of HTML which have no content in them are called as empty elements. The \
 tag used in the above example is considered to be an empty tag.

It is an empty element without a closing tag (the \
 tag defines a line break).

If you are using HTML5, you don't need to add closing tags to empty tags. But I recommend you add the closing tags anyway, as it will make your document more readable. These are also known as void elements.

Chapter 2:
Attributes

Up until now, we have only dealt with simple tags. In HTML, there are a few tags which can have attributes. Attributes are used for adding extra information. By adding an attribute, you can define the characteristics of an element in HTML. The attributes are added inside the opening tag of an element. Every attribute consists of two parts, the name and the value.

- The name in an attribute is the property that you want to add. For example, the font element has attributes like size and color with which you can define the size and color of the font. The paragraph tag has the align attribute which lets you to set the alignment of that paragraph.

- The value is something the property takes and sets into the content. For example, you can provide the size attribute with a number.

The names and values of attributes are case-sensitive and care should be taken when using them. Here is an example in which we use the align attribute for setting the alignment of the paragraph tag.

Example

<!DOCTYPE html>

<html>

<head>

<title>Align Attribute Example</title>

```
</head>
<body>
<p align="left">This paragraph is aligned left.</p>
<p align="center">This paragraph is aligned center.</p>
<p align="right">This paragraph is aligned right. </p>
</body>
</html>
```

The above code will display the following output.

This paragraph is aligned left.

This paragraph is aligned center.

This paragraph is aligned right.

Core attributes

There are four core attributes in HTML that are generally used. They are:

- id
- title
- class
- style

Internationalization attributes

In HTML, there are three internationalization attributes that are available for most of the XHTML elements. They are:

- dir

- lang

- xml:lang

Generic attributes

The table below gives some other attributes that can be used with most of the tags in HTML.

Attribute	Options	Function
align	right, left, center	Horizontally aligns tags
valign	top, middle, bottom	Vertically aligns tags within an HTML element
bgcolor	numeric, hexadecimal, RGB values	Places a background color behind an element
background	URL	Places a background image behind an element

id	User Defined	Names an element for use with Cascading Style Sheets
class	User Defined	Classifies an element for use with Cascading Style Sheets
width	Numeric Value	Specifies the width of tables, images, or table cells
height	Numeric Value	Specifies the height of tables, images, or table cells
title	User Defined	"Pop-up" title of the elements

Chapter 3:
Formatting

Formatting is displaying the text in different formats like bold, italic or underlined. Formatting is familiar for anyone who uses a word processor. Let's see how to do it in HTML.

Bold

Any content that is placed between the **...** elements will be shown in bold.

Example

<!DOCTYPE html>

<html>

<head>

<title>This text is bold</title>

</head>

</html>

This will produce the following result

This text is bold

Italics

Any content that is placed between the **<i>...</i>** elements will be italicized.

Example

```
<!DOCTYPE html>
<html>
<head>
<title><i>This text will be italicized</i></title>
</head>
</html>
```

This will produce the following result:

This text will be italicized

Underlined

Any content that is placed between the **<u>...</u>** elements will be underlined.

Example

```
<!DOCTYPE html>
<html>
<head>
<title><u>This text is underlined </u></title>
</head>
</html>
```

This will produce following result:

This text is underlined

Strikethrough

The content that is placed inside the element **<strike>...</strike>** will be shown as strikethrough text. Strikethrough text is text with a thin line through it.

Example

<!DOCTYPE html>

<html>

<head>

<title><strike>This text is struck</strike></title>

</head>

</html>

This will produce following result:

This text is struck

Monospace

Any content that is placed in between the **<tt>...</tt>** tags will be shown in monospaced font. The width of every character in a monospaced font is the same.

Example

<!DOCTYPE html>

<html>

<head>

<title>Monospaced Font Example</title>

```
</head>

<body>

<p>The following word uses a <tt>monospaced</tt>
typeface.</p>

</body>

</html>
```

This will produce following result:

The following word uses a monospaced typeface.

Superscript

The content placed between the **^{...}** element
will be displayed as superscript. Superscript font is smaller
than the regular font surrounding it and is displayed half a
character's height above the regular characters.

Example

```
<!DOCTYPE html>

<html>

<head>

<title>Superscript Text Example</title>

</head>

<body>

<p>The following word uses a <sup>superscript</sup>
typeface.</p>
```

```
</body>

</html>
```

This code will give us the following output.

The following word uses a superscript typeface.

Subscript

Any content that is placed inside the **_{...}** element will be shown as subscript. Subscript is like superscript but is displayed below other characters.

Example

```
<!DOCTYPE html>

<html>

<head>

<title>Subscript Text Example</title>

</head>

<body>

<p>The following word uses a <sub>subscript</sub> typeface.</p>

</body>

</html>
```

This code will give us the following output.

The following word uses a subscript typeface.

Inserted text

Any content that is placed inside the **<ins>...</ins>** element will be displayed as inserted text.

Example

<!DOCTYPE html>

<html>

<head>

<title>This is an example for Inserted Text</title>

</head>

<body>

<p>I want to eat <del>cola</del> <ins>pizza</ins></p>

</body>

</html>

This code will give as the following output.

I want to eat pizza

Deleted text

Any content that is placed within the **<del>...</del>** element will be displayed as deleted text.

Example

<!DOCTYPE html>

<html>

```
<head>

<title>Deleted Text Example</title>

</head>

<body>

<p>I want to eat <del>cola</del> <ins>pizza</ins></p>

</body>

</html>
```

This code will give us the following output.

I want to eat pizza

Larger text

Any content that is placed within the **<big>...</big>** element will be displayed as text that is one size larger than the text surrounding it.

Example

```
<!DOCTYPE html>

<html>

<head>

<title>Larger Text Example</title>

</head>

<body>

<p>The following word uses a <big>big</big> typeface.</p>
```

```
</body>
```

```
</html>
```

This code will produce the following output.

The following word uses a big typeface.

Smaller text

Any content that is placed within the **<small>...</small>** element will be displayed as text that is one size smaller than the text surrounding it. Here is an example.

Example

```
<!DOCTYPE html>
```

```
<html>
```

```
<head>
```

```
<title>Smaller Text Example</title>
```

```
</head>
```

```
<body>
```

```
<p>The following word uses a <small>small</small> typeface.</p>
```

```
</body>
```

```
</html>
```

This code will produce the following output.

The following word uses a small typeface.

Grouping content

The elements **<div>** and **<span>** are used for grouping several elements together to create subsections or sections of a given page.

For instance, you might sometimes need to put all the footnotes inside a <div> element, which indicates that all of those elements relate to the footnotes. You can also add special style rules to the <div> element.

Example

```
<!DOCTYPE html>

<html>

<head>

<title>Div Tag Example</title>

</head>

<body>

<div id="menu" align="middle" >

<a href="/index.htm">HOME</a> |

<a href="/about/contact_us.htm">CONTACT</a> |

<a href="/about/index.htm">ABOUT</a>

</div>

<div id="content" align="left" bgcolor="white">

<h5>Content Articles</h5>

<p>Actual content goes here.....</p>
```

```
</div>

</body>

</html>
```

This code will produce the following output.

HOME | CONTACT | ABOUT

CONTENT ARTICLES

Actual content goes here...

Unlike the <div> element, the <span> element can only grow in line elements together. So you can use the <span> element for grouping a sentence or paragraph.

Example

```
<!DOCTYPE html>

<html>

<head>

<title>Span Tag Example</title>

</head>

<body>

<p>This is the example of <span style="color:green">span tag</span> and the <span style="color:red">div tag</span> along with CSS.</p>

</body>

</html>
```

This code will produce the following output.

This is the example of span tag and the div tag along with CSS.

Chapter 4:
Phrase Tags

In HTML, the phrase tags are designed for specific purposes. These are similar to other basic tags like <i>, <b>, <tt>, and <pre>. In this chapter we will discuss all of the important phrase tags. Let us have a look at each of them in detail.

Emphasized text

Any content that is placed inside the **<em>...</em>** element will be shown as emphasized text.

Example

<!DOCTYPE html>

<html>

<head>

<title>Emphasized Text Example</title>

</head>

<body>

<p>The following word uses an <em>emphasized</em> typeface.</p>

</body>

</html>

This code will produce the following output.

The following word uses an *emphasized* typeface.

Marked text

Any content that is placed inside the **<mark>...</mark>** element will be shown as marked text. Marked text will be shown in yellow.

Example

```
<!DOCTYPE html>

<html>

<head>

<title>Marked Text Example</title>

</head>

<body>

<p>The following word has been <mark>marked</mark> with yellow</p>

</body>

</html>
```

This code will produce the following output.

The following word has been marked with yellow.

Strong text

Any content that is placed inside the **...** element will be shown as important text.

Example

```
<!DOCTYPE html>

<html>

<head>

<title>Strong Text Example</title>

</head>

<body>

<p>The following word uses a <strong>strong</strong> typeface.</p>

</body>

</html>
```

This code will produce the following output.

The following word uses a **strong** typeface.

Abbreviation

Text can be abbreviated by placing it inside the **<abbr>** and **</abbr>** tags. If this is present, the title attribute should only contain the full description.

Example

```
<!DOCTYPE html>

<html>

<head>

<title>Text Abbreviation</title>
```

```
</head>

<body>

<p>My     best     friend's     name     is     <abbr
title="Abigail">Abi</abbr>.</p>

</body>

</html>
```

This code will produce the following output.

My best friend's name is Abi.

Acronym element

By using the **<acronym>** and **</acronym>** element, you can show the text as an acronym. At present, however, none of the major browsers change the <acronym> element's content.

Example

```
<!DOCTYPE html>

<html>

<head>

<title>Acronym Example</title>

</head>

<body>

<p>This     chapter     covers     marking     up     text     in
<acronym>XHTML</acronym>.</p>

</body>
```

```
</html>
```

This code produces the following output.

This chapter covers marking up text in XHTML.

Text direction

The **<bdo>...</bdo>** element indicates bi-directional override. Using this will override the text direction of current text.

Example

```
<!DOCTYPE html>

<html>

<head>

<title>Text Direction Example</title>

</head>

<body>

<p>This text will go left to right.</p>

<p><bdo dir="rtl">This text will go right to left.</bdo></p>

</body>

</html>
```

This code will produce the following output.

This text will go left to right.

.tfel ot thgir og lliw txet sihT

Special terms

The **<dfn>...</dfn>** element will allow the user to specify that he will be introducing a special term. The usage of special terms is similar to italic words present in the middle of a paragraph. The <dfn>...</dfn> element will be used whenever you introduce a key term for the first time. The latest browsers render the content present in the <dfn> element in italics.

Example

<!DOCTYPE html>

<html>

<head>

<title>Special Terms Example</title>

</head>

<body>

<p>The following word is a <dfn>special</dfn> term.</p>

</body>

</html>

The code will produce the following output.

The following word is a *special* term.

Block quotes

You can use the **<blockquote>...</blockquote>** tags for quoting a passage taken from another source. This will sometimes use italicized font, and it is usually indented from the right and left edges of the surrounding text.

Example

<!DOCTYPE html>

<html>

<head>

<title>Blockquote Example</title>

</head>

<body>

<p>The following description of XHTML is taken from the W3C Web site:</p>

<blockquote>XHTML 1.0 is the W3C's first Recommendation for XHTML, following on from earlier work on HTML 4.01, HTML 4.0, HTML 3.2 and HTML 2.0.</blockquote>

</body>

</html>

This code will produce the following output.

The following description of XHTML is taken from the W3C Web site:

XHTML 1.0 is the W3C's first Recommendation for XHTML, following on from earlier work on HTML 4.01, HTML 4.0, HTML 3.2 and HTML 2.0.

Short quotations

If you wish to add a double quote inside a sentence, you can use the **<q>...</q>** element.

Example

<!DOCTYPE html>

<html>

<head>

<title>Double Quote Example</title>

</head>

<body>

<p>Bumblebee is in Spain, <q>I think I am wrong</q>.</p>

</body>

</html>

This code will produce the following output.

Bumblebee is in Spain, "I think I am wrong".

Text citations

You can indicate the source of the quoted text by placing it inside the opening **<cite>** tag and closing **</cite>** tag. By default, the content of this element will be rendered in italics.

36

Example

```
<!DOCTYPE html>

<html>

<head>

<title>Citations Example</title>

</head>

<body>

<p>This HTML tutorial is derived from <cite>W3 Standard for HTML</cite>.</p>

</body>

</html>
```

This code will produce the following output.

This HTML tutorial is derived from W3 Standard for HTML.

Computer code

If there is any programming code that you wish to display on your webpage, you can place that code within the **<code>...</code>** tags. Any content that is placed in this tag will be displayed as monospaced font like the text in most programming books.

Example

```
<!DOCTYPE html>

<html>
```

```
<head>

<title>Computer Code Example</title>

</head>

<body>

<p>Regular text. <code>This is code.</code> Regular
text.</p>

</body>

</html>
```

This code will produce the following output.

Regular text. This is code. Regular text.

Keyboard text

If you want to invite your reader to type some text, you can indicate what to type by using **<kbd>...</kbd>**. This is shown in the example given below.

Example

```
<!DOCTYPE html>

<html>

<head>

<title>Keyboard Text Example</title>

</head>

<body>
```

```
<p>Regular text. <kbd>This is inside kbd element</kbd>
Regular text.</p>

</body>

</html>
```

This code will produce the following output.

Regular text. This is inside kbd element Regular text.

Programming variables

If you wish to indicate that the content of a particular element is a variable, this element can be used along with the **<pre>** and **<code>**.

Example

```
<!DOCTYPE html>

<html>

<head>

<title>Variable Text Example</title>

</head>

<body>

<p><code>document.write("<var>user-name</var>")</code></p>

</body>

</html>
```

This code will produce the following output.

document.write("user-name")

Program output

For indicating a sample output of a script or a program, you can use the **<samp>...</samp>** element. This element is mostly used for showing documentation programming concepts in coding on the webpage.

Example

```
<!DOCTYPE html>

<html>

<head>

<title>Program Output Example</title>

</head>

<body>

<p>Result produced by the program is <samp>Hello World!</samp></p>

</body>

</html>
```

This code will produce the following output.

Result produced by the program is Hello World!

Address text

The **<address>...</address>** element contains an address.

Example

```
<!DOCTYPE html>
<html>
<head>
<title>Address Example</title>
</head>
<body>
<address>1818c, David Drive, Marietta – Atlanta</address>
</body>
</html>
```

This will produce following result:

1818c, David Drive, Marietta – Atlanta

Chapter 5:
Meta Tags

Metadata can be defined as the additional important information about a document in a number of ways. HTML allows its users to specify this metadata. The META elements can be used to add value/name pairs that are used to describe the HTML document properties like document or other, list of keywords, expiry date, date of creation, number of times edited etc.

They use the **<meta>** tag to provide this kind of information. This bag is an empty element, which means you don't need to add a closing tag. This tag carries the information inside its attributes. You can add more than one meta tag to your document. These tags do not change the visual appearance of the HTML document. Whether you include them or not doesn't matter to someone viewing the webpage.

Adding meta tags to your documents

You can add additional information or metadata to your webpages by using <meta> tags inside the header. In addition to the core meta attributes, the following attributes can be added to a meta tag.

Attribute	Description
Name	Name for the property. Can be anything. Examples include keywords, description, author, revised, generator etc.

Content	Specifies the property's value.
Scheme	Specifies a scheme to interpret the property's value (as declared in the content attribute).
http-equiv	Used for http response message headers. For example, http-equiv can be used to refresh the page or to set a cookie. Values include content-type, expires, refresh and set-cookie.

Specifying keywords

You can specify important keywords using the <meta> tag. They will then be used by search engines for indexing the webpage for presentation when people are searching.

In the example given below we will add HTML, meta tags and metadata as the document's important keywords.

Example

<!DOCTYPE html>

<html>

<head>

<title>Meta Tags Example</title>

<meta name="keywords" content="HTML, Meta Tags, Metadata" />

</head>

```
<body>

<p>Hello HTML5!</p>

</body>

</html>
```

This code will produce the following output.

Hello HTML5!

Document description

Using the <meta> tag, you can add a short description to your document. This description can be used by search engines when searching for your webpage.

Example

```
<!DOCTYPE html>

<html>

<head>

<title>Meta Tags Example</title>

<meta name="keywords" content="HTML, Meta Tags, Metadata" />

<meta name="description" content="Learning about Meta Tags." />

</head>

<body>

<p>Hello HTML5!</p>
```

```
</body>
```

```
</html>
```

Document revision date

The <meta> tag can be used for holding information about the last time the document was edited or updated. Web browsers use this information when refreshing your webpage.

Example

```
<!DOCTYPE html>
```

```
<html>
```

```
<head>
```

```
<title>Meta Tags Example</title>
```

```
<meta name="keywords" content="HTML, Meta Tags, Metadata" />
```

```
<meta name="description" content="Learning about Meta Tags." />
```

```
<meta name="revised" content="Tutorialspoint, 3/7/2014" />
```

```
</head>
```

```
<body>
```

```
<p>Hello HTML5!</p>
```

```
</body>
```

```
</html>
```

Document refresh

You can direct the browser to refresh the webpage after a specific period of time using a <meta> tag. The browser will continuously refresh your webpage automatically.

In this example, the browser will refresh your webpage every 10 seconds.

Example

```
<!DOCTYPE html>

<html>

<head>

<title>Meta Tags Example</title>

<meta name="keywords" content="HTML, Meta Tags, Metadata" />

<meta name="description" content="Learning about Meta Tags." />

<meta name="revised" content="Google, 3/7/2014" />

<meta http-equiv="refresh" content="10" />

</head>

<body>

<p>Hello HTML5!</p>

</body>

</html>
```

Page redirection

Sometimes you might need to redirect the browser to some other webpage. In such situations, you can use the<meta> tag for redirecting to a specific webpage. You can also tell the browser to redirect after waiting for a certain period of time calculated in seconds.

The following is an example of redirecting the current page to another page after 15 seconds. If you want to redirect the page immediately then do not specify content attribute.

Example

```
<!DOCTYPE html>

<html>

<head>

<title>Meta Tags Example</title>

<meta name="keywords" content="HTML, Meta Tags, Metadata" />

<meta name="description" content="Learning about Meta Tags." />

<meta name="revised" content="google, 3/7/2014" />

<meta http-equiv="refresh" content="15; url=http://www.google.com" />

</head>

<body>

<p>Hello HTML5!</p>
```

```
</body>
```

```
</html>
```

Setting cookies

Cookies are data that is stored in small text files on your computer. They are exchanged between the web server and your web browser. Cookies help to keep track of information that the web application might need. You can store these cookies on the client server or the client side using the <meta> tag. This same information will later be used by the web servers for keeping records of the client's visit.

In the example given below, the cookie will be considered a session cookie if the expiration time and date are not specified. This cookie will be allocated or deleted when the session expires.

Example

```
<!DOCTYPE html>
```

```
<html>
```

```
<head>
```

```
<title>Meta Tags Example</title>
```

```
<meta name="keywords" content="HTML, Meta Tags, Metadata" />
```

```
<meta name="description" content="Learning about Meta Tags." />
```

```
<meta name="revised" content="Google, 3/7/2014" />
```

```
<meta          http-equiv="cookie"          content="userid=xyz;
expires=Wednesday, 08-Aug-15 23:59:59 GMT;" />

</head>

<body>

<p>Hello HTML5!</p>

</body>

</html>
```

Setting author name

Using the <meta> tag, you can specify the author name in your webpage.

Example

```
<!DOCTYPE html>

<html>

<head>

<title>Meta Tags Example</title>

<meta    name="keywords"    content="HTML,    Meta    Tags,
Metadata" />

<meta  name="description"  content="Learning  about  Meta
Tags." />

<meta name="author" content="Rafael Nadal" />

</head>

<body>
```

```
<p>Hello HTML5!</p>
```

```
</body>
```

```
</html>
```

Specify character set

Using the <meta> tag, you can specify the character set that is used in your webpage.

By default, web browsers and servers use ISo–8859–1 encoding to process webpages. The example given below will use the set UTF-8 encoding.

Example

```
<!DOCTYPE html>
```

```
<html>
```

```
<head>
```

```
<title>Meta Tags Example</title>
```

```
<meta name="keywords" content="HTML, Meta Tags, Metadata" />
```

```
<meta name="description" content="Learning about Meta Tags." />
```

```
<meta name="author" content="Rafael Nadal" />
```

```
<meta http-equiv="Content-Type" content="text/html; charset=UTF-8" />
```

```
</head>
```

```
<body>
```

```html
<p>Hello HTML5!</p>

</body>

</html>
```

Chinese characters

For serving a static page which contains traditional Chinese characters, Big5 encoding must be used in the <meta> tag.

Example

```html
<!DOCTYPE html>

<html>

<head>

<title>Meta Tags Example</title>

<meta name="keywords" content="HTML, Meta Tags, Metadata" />

<meta name="description" content="Learning about Meta Tags." />

<meta name="author" content="Optimus Prime" />

<meta http-equiv="Content-Type" content="text/html; charset=Big5" />

</head>

<body>

<p>Hello HTML5!</p>

</body>

</html>
```

Chapter 6:
Comments

Comments are pieces of code that the web browser will ignore. It is recommended that you add comments, especially when writing complex HTML documents, to indicate the sections in the document. Comments will help you and any other user looking at your HTML document, so it is always a good practice to add them. Comments will make the code more readable, which in turn helps you and others to get a better understanding of your code.

In HTML, the content placed within **<!-- ... -->** tags will be considered as a comment and the web browser will ignore it completely.

Example

<!DOCTYPE html>

<html>

<head> <!-- Document Header Starts -->

<title>This is document title</title>

</head> <!-- Document Header Ends -->

<body>

<p>Document content goes here...</p>

</body>

</html>

The above code will give us the following output and the text placed within <!-- ... --> tags will be ignored.

Document content goes here...

Valid vs. invalid comments

HTML does not support nesting of comments. This means that you cannot place a comment within another comment. You should ensure that there are no spaces in the beginning of the comment string. Given below are two examples in which valid and invalid comments are used.

Valid

The comment given in this first example is valid and will be completely ignored by the browser.

Example

<!DOCTYPE html>

<html>

<head>

<title>Valid Comment Example</title>

</head>

<body>

<!-- This is a valid comment -->

<p> Document content goes here...</p>

</body>

```
</html>
```

The comment in the below example is not a valid comment and the browser will display it. This comment is not valid because of the space between the left bracket and the exclamation point.

Example

```
<!DOCTYPE html>

<html>

<head>

<title>Invalid Comment Example</title>

</head>

<body>

< !-- This is not a valid comment -->

<p> Document content goes here...</p>

</body>

</html>
```

The above code will give us the following output:

< !-- This is not a valid comment -->

Document content goes here...

Multiline comments

Up until now, we have only discussed single line comments. However, HTML also supports multi-line comments.

You can add multiple lines as comments by using the beginning tag **<!--** and ending tag **-->**. These should be placed above the first line and after the end of the last line.

Example

<!DOCTYPE html><html>

<head>

<title>Multiline Comments</title>

</head>

<body>

<!--

This is a multiline comment and it can

span as many as lines you like.

-->

<p>Document content goes here...</p>

</body>

</html>

Is code will produce the following output.

Document content goes here...

Conditional comments

Conditional comments are only effective with the Internet Explorer browser. Other browsers will simply ignore them. You can use conditional comments to give conditional instructions to the Internet Explorer browser.

Example

```
<!DOCTYPE html><html>

<head>

<title>Conditional Comments</title>

<!--[if IE 6]>

Special instructions for IE 6 here

<![endif]-->

</head>

<body>

<p>Document content goes here...</p>

</body>

</html>
```

You may find yourself in situations where you will need to use a different style sheet depending on the version of Internet Explorer used. Conditional comments can be helpful in such situations.

Using the <comment> tag

Only a few of the available browsers support the <comment> tag. This tag is used to add comments in your HTML code.

Example

<!DOCTYPE html><html>

<head>

<title>Using Comment Tag</title>

</head>

<body>

<p>This is <comment>not</comment> Internet Explorer.</p>

</body>

</html>

If you are using IE this will produce the following result:

This is Internet Explorer.

But if you are not using IE, then it will produce this result:

This is not Internet Explorer.

Commenting style sheets

Here, we will use a cascading style sheet in your HTML code. For the present, you should just note that these should be properly placed inside HTML comments. We will discuss cascading style sheets more fully in later chapters.

Example

```
<!DOCTYPE html><html>
<head>
<title>Commenting Style Sheets</title>
<style>
<!--
.example {
 border:1px solid #4a7d49;
}
//-->
</style>
</head>
<body>
<div class="example">Hi there!</div>
</body>
</html>
```

This code will produce the following output

Hi there!

Chapter 7:
Images

In HTML, images play a very important role in conveying your message. They are also important to beautify your webpage. Many complex concepts can be depicted in a simple manner by using images. In this tutorial, we will learn how to use images on your webpages.

Inserting an image

You can add an image to your webpage with the <img> tag.

The syntax for using this simple tag is:

<img src="Image URL" ... attributes-list/>

This tag is an empty one, which means that you can only give the list of attributes and it will not have a closing tag.

Now, let's try the below example. Our HTML file will be tested.htm and the image file will be test.png. Both of these files will be present in the same directory.

Example

<!DOCTYPE html>

<html>

<head>

<title>Using Image in Webpage</title>

</head>

<body>

<p>Simple Image Insert</p>

<img src="/html/images/test.png" alt="Test Image" />

</body>

</html>

The above code will produce the following output.

Simple Image Insert

HTML supports JPEG, PNG and GIF images. The correct image file name should be specified in the src attribute. Always keep in mind that image names are case sensitive.

There is a mandatory attribute called the alt attribute, which will specify alternate text for a given image for use in cases where the image cannot be displayed.

Setting image location

It is wise to use a separate directory for your images. We will save our HTML file text.htm in the home directory. Inside the home directory, you can create a directory for images and you can store the image test.png. We will try the below example assuming the image location to be /html/image/test.png.

Example

```
<!DOCTYPE html>
<html>
<head>
<title>Using Image in Webpage</title>
</head>
<body>
<p>Simple Image Insert</p>
<img src="/html/images/test.png" alt="Test Image" />
</body>
</html>
```

The above code will produce the following output.

Simple Image Insert

Setting image height/width

You can set the width and height of an image based on your requirements using the width and height attributes. These attributes can be specified in terms of their percentage of the image's actual size or in terms of pixels.

Example

<!DOCTYPE html>

<html>

<head>

<title>Set Image Width and Height</title>

</head>

<body>

<p>Setting image width and height</p>

<img src="/html/images/test.png" alt="Test Image" width="150" height="100"/>

</body>

</html>

The above code will produce an image with a height of 100 pixels and a width of 150 pixels.

Setting image border

By default every image will have a border around it. By using the border attribute, you can specify the thickness in pixels. If the thickness of 0 is given to an image, no border will be added.

Example

```
<!DOCTYPE html>

<html>

<head>

<title>Set Image Border</title>

</head>

<body>

<p>Setting image Border</p>

<img    src="/html/images/test.png"    alt="Test    Image"
border="3"/>

</body>

</html>
```

The above code will produce an output image with a border size of three pixels.

Setting image alignment

By default all images will be aligned to the left. You can use the align attribute to put them at the right or center.

Example

```
<!DOCTYPE html>

<html>

<head>

<title>Set Image Alignment</title>
```

</head>

<body>

<p>Setting image Alignment</p>

<img   src="/html/images/test.png"   alt="Test   Image"
border="3" align="right"/>

</body>

</html>

The above code will produce an output image aligned to the right side of the webpage:

Chapter 8:
Tables

HTML users can insert tables in their webpages. A table in HTML can contain data like images, text, links and even other tables. This data will be placed inside the rows and columns of cells. Tables can be created by using the **<table>** tag. For creating new rows we use the **<tr>** tag, and the **<td>** tag is for creating data cells.

Example

<!DOCTYPE html>

<html>

<head>

<title>HTML Tables</title>

</head>

<body>

<table border="1">

<tr>

<td>R1, C1</td>

<td>R1, C2</td>

</tr>

<tr>

<td>R2, C1</td>

<td>R2, C2</td>

</tr>

</table>

</body>

</html>

This will produce the following result:

R1, C1	R1, C2
R2, C1	R2, C2

The table tag has an attribute called border that will add a border to all the cells. If you don't need a border, you can set the value to 0.

Table heading

You can define the heading of a table using the **<th>** tag. This tag will be a replacement for the <td> tag which represents the cell data. The <th> tag is usually placed on the top row as the table heading; otherwise the <td> element can be used in any row.

Example

<!DOCTYPE html>

<html>

<head>

66

```html
<title>HTML Table Header</title>
</head>
<body>
<table border="1">
<tr>
<th>Name</th>
<th>Salary</th>
</tr>
<tr>
<td>LeBron James</td>
<td>5000</td>
</tr>
<tr>
<td>Roger Federer</td>
<td>7000</td>
</tr>
</table>
</body>
</html>
```

This will produce the following result:

Name	Salary
LeBron James	5000
Roger Federer	7000

Cellpadding & cellspacing attributes

You can set the white space in your table cells using the cellpadding and cellspacing attributes.

The cellspacing attribute is used for defining the border width and the cellpadding attribute represents the pixel distance between two cell borders and the content within.

Example

```
<!DOCTYPE html>

<html>

<head>

<title>HTML Table Cellpadding</title>

</head>

<body>

<table border="1" cellpadding="5" cellspacing="5">

<tr>
```

```
<th>Name</th>
<th>Salary</th>
</tr>
<tr>
<td>Robin Williams</td>
<td>5000</td>
</tr>
<tr>
<td>Cristiano Ronaldo</td>
<td>7000</td>
</tr>
</table>
</body>
</html>
```

This code will produce the following output table:

Name	Salary
Robin Williams	5000
Cristiano Ronaldo	7000

Colspan & rowspan attributes

You can merge two or more columns in a table to a single column using the colspan attribute.

Similarly, for combining two or more rows into a single row you use the attribute called rowspan.

Example

```
<!DOCTYPE html>

<html>

<head>

<title>HTML Table Colspan/Rowspan</title>

</head>

<body>

<table border="1">

<tr>

<th>Column 1</th>

<th>Column 2</th>

<th>Column 3</th>

</tr>

<tr><td rowspan="2">Row 1 Cell 1</td><td>Row 1 Cell 2</td><td>Row 1 Cell 3</td></tr>

<tr><td>Row 2 Cell 2</td><td>Row 2 Cell 3</td></tr>

<tr><td colspan="3">Row 3 Cell 1</td></tr>
```

```
</table>

</body>

</html>
```

This will produce the following result:

Column 1	Column 2	Column 3
Row 1 Cell 1	Row 1 Cell 2	Row 1 Cell 3
	Row 2 Cell 2	Row 2 Cell 3
Row 3 Cell 1		

Tables backgrounds

By default, all tables have white as their background color. You can change the background color or even add an image as a background in a table. For changing the background of a given table you can follow either of these two methods:

- bgcolor attribute – Using this attribute, you can set the background color for a single cell or for the whole table.

- background attribute – This attribute will allow you to set an image as a background for a single cell or for the whole table.

The color of the border for a table can be changed by using an attribute called bordercolor.

Example

```
<!DOCTYPE html>
<html>
<head>
<title>HTML Table Background</title>
</head>
<body>
<table border="1" bordercolor="green" bgcolor="yellow">
<tr>
<th>Column 1</th>
<th>Column 2</th>
<th>Column 3</th>
</tr>
<tr><td rowspan="2">Row 1 Cell 1</td><td>Row 1 Cell 2</td><td>Row 1 Cell 3</td></tr>
<tr><td>Row 2 Cell 2</td><td>Row 2 Cell 3</td></tr>
<tr><td colspan="3">Row 3 Cell 1</td></tr>
</table>
</body>
</html>
```

This will produce the following result:

Column 1	Column 2	Column 3
Row 1 Cell 1	Row 1 Cell 2	Row 1 Cell 3
	Row 2 Cell 2	Row 2 Cell 3
Row 3 Cell 1		

In the following example, we will use an image from the local directory as the background of the table. This can be done by using the background attribute.

Example

<!DOCTYPE html>

<html>

<head>

<title>HTML Table Background</title>

</head>

<body>

<table border="1" border color="green" background="/images/test.png">

<tr>

<th>Column 1</th>

<th>Column 2</th>

```
<th>Column 3</th>

</tr>

<tr><td rowspan="2">Row 1 Cell 1</td><td>Row 1 Cell
2</td><td>Row 1 Cell 3</td></tr>

<tr><td>Row 2 Cell 2</td><td>Row 2 Cell 3</td></tr>

<tr><td colspan="3">Row 3 Cell 1</td></tr>

</table>

</body>

</html>
```

This will add the image test.png as the background for the table.

Table caption

You can use the **<caption>** tag for displaying the title or an explanation to a table. This will be on top of the table. In the latest versions of HTML/XHTML, this is deprecated.

Example

```
<!DOCTYPE html>

<html>

<head>

<title>HTML Table Caption</title>

</head>

<body>
```

```
<table border="1" width="100%">

<caption>This is the caption</caption>

<tr>

<td>row 1, column 1</td><td>row 1, column 2</td>

</tr>

<tr>

<td>row 2, column 1</td><td>row 2, column 2</td>

</tr>

</table>

</body>

</html>
```

This code will give us the following output:

row 1, column 1	row 1, column 2
row 2, column 1	row 2, column 2

Table header, body & footer

Every table contains three parts. They are the header, the body and the footer. The header and the footer are similar to the headers and footers that are present in word processors. Headers and footers remain the same for every page. The main content of the table is placed in the body.

You can actually separate the header, body and footer of the table using the three elements given below.

- **<thead>** – This will create a table header separately.

- **<tbody>** – This is used for indicating the main body of the given table.

- **<tfoot>** – This is used for creating a table footer separately.

The table can contain any number of <tbody> elements that indicate groups or pages of data. The <thead> tag and the <tfoot> tag should only be placed before the <tbody> tag.

Example

```
<!DOCTYPE html>

<html>

<head>

<title>HTML Table</title>

</head>

<body>

<table border="1" width="100%">

<thead>

<tr>

<td colspan="4">This is the head of the table</td>

</tr>

</thead>
```

```html
<tfoot>
<tr>
<td colspan="4">This is the foot of the table</td>
</tr>
</tfoot>
<tbody>
<tr>
<td>Cell 1</td>
<td>Cell 2</td>
<td>Cell 3</td>
<td>Cell 4</td>
</tr>
</tbody>
</table>
</body>
</html>
```

This code will give us the following output:

This is the head of the table			
This is the foot of the table			
Cell 1	Cell 2	Cell 3	Cell 4

Nested tables

In HTML, it is possible to place a table inside another table. Such tables are known as nested tables. This is not just limited to adding tables; almost all of the tags can be placed inside a given table data tag <td>.

In the following example we are adding another table inside the table cell.

Example

<!DOCTYPE html>

<html>

<head>

<title>HTML Table</title>

</head>

<body>

<table border="1" width="100%">

<tr>

78

```html
<td>
  <table border="1" width="100%">
  <tr>
  <th>Name</th>
  <th>Salary</th>
  </tr>
  <tr>
  <td>Bruce Lee</td>
  <td>4000</td>
  </tr>
  <tr>
  <td> George Clooney</td>
  <td>6000</td>
  </tr>
  </table>
</td>
</tr>
</table>
</body>
</html>
```

This code will give us the following output:

Name	Salary
Bruce Lee	4000
George Clooney	6000

Chapter 9:
Lists

HTML offers three ways to specify lists of information.

\<ul\> – This is an unordered list where the items will be listed with plain bullets.

\<ol\> – This is an ordered list, which uses different schemes of numbers for listing items.

\<dl\> – This is a definition list. The definition list will arrange the items as they would be in a dictionary.

Unordered list

An unordered list can be defined as a collection of related items with no special sequence or order. An unordered list can be created by making use of the \<ul\> tag. Every item present in the list will be marked with a bullet.

Example

\<!DOCTYPE html\>

\<html\>

\<head\>

\<title\>HTML Unordered List\</title\>

\</head\>

\<body\>

\<ul\>

```
<li>BMW</li>
<li>Nissan</li>
<li>Jaguar</li>
<li>Mercedes</li>
</ul>
</body>
</html>
```

The above code will produce the following output.

- BMW

- Nissan

- Jaguar

- Mercedes

The type attribute

You can use the type attribute in a <ul> tag to specify the type of bullet you want. The default bullet is a disc. The possible options are given below:

```
<ul type="square">
```

```
<ul type="disc">
```

```
<ul type="circle">
```

In the below example, we will use the <ul type="square">.

Example

```
<!DOCTYPE html>
<html>
<head>
<title>HTML Unordered List</title>
</head>
<body>
  <ul type="square">
<li>BMW</li>
<li>Nissan</li>
<li>Jaguar</li>
<li>Mercedes</li>
</ul>
</body>
</html>
```

The above code will produce the following result:

- BMW

- Nissan

- Jaguar

- Mercedes

In this example we will use the <ul type="disc">.

Example

```
<!DOCTYPE html>
<html>
<head>
<title>HTML Unordered List</title>
</head>
<body>
  <ul type="disc">
<li>BMW</li>
<li>Nissan</li>
<li>Jaguar</li>
<li>Mercedes</li>   </ul>
</body>
</html>
```

This will produce following result:

- BMW

- Nissan

- Jaguar

- Mercedes

In this example we will use the <ul type="circle">.

Example

```
<!DOCTYPE html>
<html>
<head>
<title>HTML Unordered List</title>
</head>
<body>
  <ul type="circle">
  <li>BMW</li>
  <li>Nissan</li>
  <li>Jaguar</li>
  <li>Mercedes</li>
  </ul>
</body>
</html>
```

The above code will produce the following output:

- o   BMW

- o   Nissan

- o   Jaguar

- o   Mercedes

Ordered lists

In some cases, you will want to list items by number rather than using bullets. In such cases, you can use an ordered list. An ordered list can be created with the <ol> tag. The numbers start with one and are incremented with every successive element that is tagged with <li>.

Example

<!DOCTYPE html>

<html>

<head>

<title>HTML Ordered List</title>

</head>

<body>

<ol>

<li>BMW</li>

<li>Nissan</li>

<li>Jaguar</li>

<li>Mercedes</li>

</ol>

</body>

</html>

The above code will produce the following output:

1. BMW

2. Nissan

3. Jaguar

4. Mercedes

The type attribute

Every ordered list, by default, contains numbers. You can specify the type of numbering by using the type attribute. The possible options are given below:

<ol type="1"> - Default-Case Numerals.

<ol type="I"> - Upper-Case Numerals.

<ol type="i"> - Lower-Case Numerals.

<ol type="a"> - Lower-Case Letters.

<ol type="A"> - Upper-Case Letters.

In the below example, the <ol type="1"> is used.

Example

<!DOCTYPE html>

<html>

<head>

<title>HTML Ordered List</title>

</head>

<body>

```html
<ol type="1">
<li>BMW</li>
<li>Nissan</li>
<li>Jaguar</li>
<li>Mercedes</li>
</ol>
</body>
</html>
```

This code will produce the following output:

1. BMW

2. Nissan

3. Jaguar

4. Mercedes

In the below example, the <ol type="I"> is used.

Example

```html
<!DOCTYPE html>
<html>
<head>
<title>HTML Ordered List</title>
</head>
<body>
```

```html
<ol type="I">
<li>BMW</li>
<li>Nissan</li>
<li>Jaguar</li>
<li>Mercedes</li>
</ol>
</body>
</html>
```

The above code will produce the following output.

I. BMW

II. Nissan

III. Jaguar

IV. Mercedes

In the below example, the <ol type="i"> is used.

Example

```html
<!DOCTYPE html>
<html>
<head>
<title>HTML Ordered List</title>
</head>
<body>
```

```html
<ol type="i">
<li>BMW</li>
<li>Nissan</li>
<li>Jaguar</li>
<li>Mercedes</li>
</ol>
</body>
</html>
```

The above code will produce the following output:

i. BMW

ii. Nissan

iii. Jaguar

iv. Mercedes

In the below example, the <ol type="A"> is used.

Example

```html
<!DOCTYPE html>
<html>
<head>
<title>HTML Ordered List</title>
</head>
<body>
```

```html
<ol type="A">
<li>BMW</li>
<li>Nissan</li>
<li>Jaguar</li>
<li>Mercedes</li>
</ol>
</body>
</html>
```

The above code will produce the following output:

A. BMW

B. Nissan

C. Jaguar

D. Mercedes

In the below example, we will use the <ol type="a">.

Example

```html
<!DOCTYPE html>
<html>
<head>
<title>HTML Ordered List</title>
</head>
<body>
```

```
<ol type="a">

<li>BMW</li>

<li>Nissan</li>

<li>Jaguar</li>

<li>Mercedes</li>

</ol>

</body>

</html>
```

The above code will produce the following output:

a. BMW

b. Nissan

c. Jaguar

d. Mercedes

The start attribute

The starting point of the numbering can be specified by using the start attribute in the <ol> tag. The possible options are given below:

<ol type="1" start="4">– Numerals starting with 4.

<ol type="I" start="4">– Numerals starting with IV.

<ol type="i" start="4">– Numerals starting with iv.

<ol type="a" start="4">– Letters starting with d.

<ol type="A" start="4">– Letters starting with D.

In the below example, <ol type="i" start="4" > is used.

Example

```
<!DOCTYPE html>
<html>
<head>
<title>HTML Ordered List</title>
</head>
<body>
 <ol type="i" start="4">
 <li>BMW</li>
 <li>Nissan</li>
 <li>Jaguar</li>
 <li>Mercedes</li>
 </ol>
</body>
</html>
```

The above code will produce the following output.

iv.   BMW

v.   Nissan

vi.   Jaguar

vii.   Mercedes

Definition lists

Both XHTML and HTML support a style of list called a definition list. All the entries in the definition list will be listed like in an encyclopedia or dictionary. Definition lists are an ideal way to present a list of terms, glossary, or other name/value list.

The following tags are used in a definition list:

- **<dl>**– The start of the list is defined by this.

- **<dt>**– A term

- **<dd>**– Term definition

- **</dl>**– Defines the end of the list

Example

<!DOCTYPE html>

<html>

<head>

<title>HTML Definition List</title>

</head>

<body>

<dl>

<dt>HTML</dt>

<dd>This stands for Hyper Text Markup Language</dd>

94

```
<dt><b>HTTP</b></dt>

<dd>This stands for Hyper Text Transfer Protocol</dd>

</dl>

</body>

</html>
```

The above code will produce the following output:

HTML

This stands for Hyper Text Markup Language

HTTP

This stands for Hyper Text Transfer Protocol

Chapter 8:
Colors

Colors play a very important role in representing your website. Using the right colors to give it a good look and feel can help attract more users. Colors can be specified on page levels with the **<body>** tag. You can use the bgcolorattribute for setting colors for individual tags.

The <body> tag has the following attributes with which different colors can be set:

- bgcolor – sets a color for the background of the page.

- text – sets a color for the body text.

- alink – sets a color for active links or selected links.

- link – sets a color for linked text.

- vlink – sets a color for visited links, that is, for linked text that you have already clicked on.

Color coding methods

In HTML, you can change the colors of the webpage using any of the three methods given below:

- Color names – The color names can be specified directly, as red, blue or green.

- Hex codes – Hex codes, otherwise known as hexadecimal codes, are six-digit codes which represent the colors.

- Color decimal or percentage values – This value can be given using the rgb( ) property.

Now, we will look at each of these schemes in detail.

Color names

When you are giving a color to your background, you can specify it directly using its name. There are a total of 16 basic colors that are listed by the World Wide Web Consortium (W3C). These are supported by almost all modern browsers. Some major browsers support up to 200 different colors.

Here is a table of the 16 standard W3C colors and their names. It is recommended that these colors are used as they are supported by most browsers.

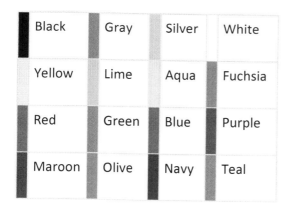

	Black		Gray		Silver	White
	Yellow		Lime		Aqua		Fuchsia
	Red		Green		Blue		Purple
	Maroon		Olive		Navy		Teal

Here is an example in which the background of the HTML tag is set using its name.

Example

```
<!DOCTYPE html>

<html>

<head>

<title>HTML Colors by Name</title>

</head>

<body text="blue" bgcolor="green">

<p>Use different color names for body and table and see the result.</p>

<table bgcolor="black">

<tr>

<td>

<font color="white">This text will appear white on black background.</font>

</td>

</tr>

</table>

</body>

</html>
```

Hex codes

A color can be represented in hexadecimal in HTML. Hexadecimal is a color representation in 6 digits. RRGGBB can be defined as 6 digits so that the first two digits take the red values, the second two digits take the green values and the last two digits are assigned for the blue.

The hexadecimal value of any color can be taken from any graphics-related software like MS Paint, Adobe Photoshop, etc. Each color value in hexadecimal will be preceded by a "#".

Color	Color HEX
	#000000
	#FF0000
	#00FF00
	#0000FF
	#FFFF00
	#00FFFF
	#FF00FF
	#C0C0C0
	#FFFFFF

Let's look at how to set the background color by using the hexadecimal color code.

Example

```
<!DOCTYPE html>
<html>
<head>
<title>HTML Colors by Hex</title>
</head>
<body text="#0000FF" bgcolor="#00FF00">
<p>Use different color hexa for body and table and see the result.</p>
<table bgcolor="#000000">
<tr>
<td>
<font color="#FFFFFF">This text will appear white on black background.</font>
</td>
</tr>
</table>
</body>
</html>
```

RGB values

These colors are specified with the rgb() property. Here, RGB means red, green and blue. These values range from 0 and

255. Instead of giving the range from 0 to 255, the percentage can also be defined when selecting a particular color. However, the rgb() property is not supported by all browsers, so its use is not recommended.

The following is a list showing a few colors using RGB values:

Color	Color RGB
	rgb(0,0,0)
	rgb(255,0,0)
	rgb(0,255,0)
	rgb(0,0,255)
	rgb(255,255,0)
	rgb(0,255,255)
	rgb(255,0,255)
	rgb(192,192,192)
	rgb(255,255,255)

In this example, we will set the background of a HTML tag using the color code values in rgb().

Example

```
<!DOCTYPE html>

<html>

<head>

<title>HTML Colors by RGB code</title>

</head>

<body text="rgb(0,0,255)" bgcolor="rgb(0,255,0)">

<p>Use different color code for body and table and see the result.</p>

<table bgcolor="rgb(0,0,0)">

<tr>

<td>

<font color="rgb(255,255,255)">This text will appear white on black background.</font>

</td>

</tr>

</table>

</body>

</html>
```

Browser safe colors

The list of all safe colors that can be used on any browser or computer is given below. In total, there are 216 safe colors available. The minimum and maximum range of these colors is 000000 to FFFFFF. The computer should support the 256 color palette for these colors to be used.

	000033	000066	000099	0000CC	0000FF
003300	003333	003366	003399	0033CC	0033FF
006600	006633	006666	006699	0066CC	0066FF
009900	009933	009966	009999	0099CC	0099FF
00CC00	00CC33	00CC66	00CC99	00CCCC	00CCFF
00FF00	00FF33	00FF66	00FF99	00FFCC	00FFFF
330000	330033	330066	330099	3300CC	3300FF
333300	333333	333366	333399	3333CC	3333FF
336600	336633	336666	336699	3366CC	3366FF
339900	339933	339966	339999	3399CC	3399FF
33CC00	33CC33	33CC66	33CC99	33CCCC	33CCFF
33FF00	33FF33	33FF66	33FF99	33FFCC	33FFFF
660000	660033	660066	660099	6600CC	6600FF

663300	663333	663366	663399	6633CC	6633FF
666600	666633	666666	666699	6666CC	6666FF
669900	669933	669966	669999	6699CC	6699FF
66CC00	66CC33	66CC66	66CC99	66CCCC	66CCFF
66FF00	66FF33	66FF66	66FF99	66FFCC	66FFFF
990000	990033	990066	990099	9900CC	9900FF
993300	993333	993366	993399	9933CC	9933FF
996600	996633	996666	996699	9966CC	9966FF
999900	999933	999966	999999	9999CC	9999FF
99CC00	99CC33	99CC66	99CC99	99CCCC	99CCFF
99FF00	99FF33	99FF66	99FF99	99FFCC	99FFFF
CC0000	CC0033	CC0066	CC0099	CC00CC	CC00FF
CC3300	CC3333	CC3366	CC3399	CC33CC	CC33FF
CC6600	CC6633	CC6666	CC6699	CC66CC	CC66FF
CC9900	CC9933	CC9966	CC9999	CC99CC	CC99FF

CCCC00	CCCC33	CCCC66	CCCC99	CCCCCC	CCCCFF
CCFF00	CCFF33	CCFF66	CCFF99	CCFFCC	CCFFFF
FF0000	FF0033	FF0066	FF0099	FF00CC	FF00FF
FF3300	FF3333	FF3366	FF3399	FF33CC	FF33FF
FF6600	FF6633	FF6666	FF6699	FF66CC	FF66FF
FF9900	FF9933	FF9966	FF9999	FF99CC	FF99FF
FFCC00	FFCC33	FFCC66	FFCC99	FFCCCC	FFCCFF
FFFF00	FFFF33	FFFF66	FFFF99	FFFFCC	FFFFFF

Chapter 10:
Links

A webpage can contain links which redirect you to other webpages or sometimes to specific parts in a particular page. These links are termed hyperlinks.

Using hyperlinks, the users visiting your webpage navigate to different websites by clicking on images, phrases or words. Hyperlinks can be created using images or text present on a webpage.

Linking documents

We will use the HTML tag **<a>** to specify a link. This is defined as the anchor tag. Anything placed between the <a> tag and the </a> tag will become a part of the link. Users clicking on this link will be redirected to the specified linked document. Syntax for using a simple <a> tag is given below:

<a href="Document URL" ... attributes-list>Link Text</a>

Now, we will try an example that will link to http://www.google.com at your page:

Example

<!DOCTYPE html>

<html>

<head>

<title>Hyperlink Example</title>

</head>

```
<body>
```

```
<p>Click following link</p>
```

```
<a href="http://www.google.com" target="_self">Google</a>
```

```
</body>
```

```
</html>
```

The above code will produce an output link and by clicking on it you will be redirected to the Google homepage.

The target attribute

We have already used the target attribute, which is used to specify the location at which a linked document is opened.

The possible options are given below:

Option	Description
_blank	This will open the linked document in a new tab or new window.
_self	This will open the given link to the document within the current frame.
_parent	The linked document will be opened in the parent frame.
_top	The linked document will be opened in the

	full body of a window.
targetframe	The linked document will be opened in a *targetframe*

Look at the below example to get a basic understanding of the differences in options provided for the target attribute.

Example

<!DOCTYPE html>

<html>

<head>

<title>Hyperlink Example</title>

<base href="http://www.tutorialspoint.com/">

</head>

<body>

<p>Click any of the following links</p>

<a href="/html/index.htm" target="_blank">Opens in New</a> |

<a href="/html/index.htm" target="_self">Opens in Self</a> |

<a href="/html/index.htm" target="_parent">Opens in Parent</a> |

```
<a    href="/html/index.htm"    target="_top">Opens    in
Body</a>
```

```
</body>
```

```
</html>
```

The above code will produce an output with four different links, and each of those links will redirect you to the document in a different way.

Use of base path

When you are linking to HTML documents of the same website, you need not always give the complete URL for each link. You can use the **<base>** tag and can get rid of them. A base path can be given for all the links using this tag. The given relative path will be concatenated by your browser to the base path and the URL will be completed.

We will use the <base> tag in the following example to specify the base URL. We will later use the relative path for the links instead of using the complete URLs.

Example

```
<!DOCTYPE html>
```

```
<html>
```

```
<head>
```

```
<title>Hyperlink Example</title>
```

```
<base href="http://www.amazon.com/">
```

```
</head>
```

```
<body>
```

`<p>Click following link</p>`

`<a href="/html/index.htm" target="_blank">Electronics</a>`

```
</body>
```

```
</html>
```

The above code will produce an output where a link named Electronics will be generated, and by clicking on it you will be taken to the electronics section in the Amazon website.

Linking to a page section

Links to particular sections of given webpages can be created using the name attribute. This process involves two steps.

In the first step, you will create a link to the place where you wish be redirected on the webpage. It will be named using tags as follows:

`<h1>HTML Text Links <a name="top"></a></h1>`

In the second step, a hyperlink will be created and the place and the document will be linked.

`<a href="/html/html_text_links.htm#top">Go to the Top</a>`

The above code will produce a link and you can select the generated link Go to the Top. Clicking on the link will take you to the top of the HTML link text tutorial.

Setting link colors

Different colors can be set for links, visited links and active links. This can be done by using the link, vlink and alink attributes in the <body> tag.

Here is an example where we will see how the link, vlink and alink attributes work. Save the given code in test.htm. After saving open it in any web browser.

Example

```
<!DOCTYPE html>

<html>

<head>

<title>Hyperlink Example</title>

<base href="http://www.tutorialspoint.com/">

</head>

<body alink="#54A250" link="#040404" vlink="#F40633">

<p>Click following link</p>

<a    href="/html/index.htm"    target="_blank"    >HTML
Tutorial</a>

</body>

</html>
```

The output link will be in one color and clicking it will change the color. Check the color of the link after activating it and after visiting it.

Download links

You can create a downloadable link so your visitors can download ZIP, DOC or PDF files. This is actually easy: all you need to do is to give the downloadable file's complete URL as in the example below.

Example

```
<!DOCTYPE html>

<html>

<head>

<title>Hyperlink Example</title>

</head>

<a     href="http://www.filehippo.com/page.pdf">Download PDF File</a>

</body>

</html>
```

The above code will produce a link and by clicking on it you can download a PDF file.

File download dialog box

In some cases, instead of displaying the content immediately, you should provide the user with an option where a download box will pop up. This is a very simple process and can be achieved by using an HTTP header in your HTTP response.

For instance, if you wish to make the file "FileName" downloadable from a link, you can use the below syntax.

Syntax

```perl
#!/usr/bin/perl

# Addtional HTTP Header

print                "Content-Type:application/octet-stream;
name=\"FileName\"\r\n";

print           "Content-Disposition:           attachment;
filename=\"FileName\"\r\n\n";

# Open the target file and list down its content as follows

open( FILE, "<FileName" );

while(read(FILE, $buffer, 100)){

 print("$buffer");

}
```

Image links

As we have already discussed, we can use images as hyperlinks. We have already seen how to add text as a hyperlink, and we have also discussed how to add images. Now we will see how images can be added as hyperlinks.

It is really easy to set an image as hyperlink. It can be done by replacing the text inside the hyperlink with an image.

Example

```html
<!DOCTYPE html>

<html>

<head>
```

```
<title>Image Hyperlink Example</title>

</head>

<body>

<p>Click following link</p>

<a href="http://www.tutorialspoint.com" target="_self">

  <img   src="/images/logo.png"   alt="Tutorials   Point"
border="0"/>

</a>

</body>

</html>
```

The above code will produce an output which generates an image, and by clicking on it you will be redirected to a different page.

This is a simple example where an image is used as a hyperlink. Next, we'll learn to create mouse-sensitive image links.

Mouse-sensitive images

HTML and XHTML provide a feature that allows different links to be embedded inside a single image according to the different coordinates of the image. After you attach different links to the different coordinates, clicking on different parts of the image will open different target documents. These mouse-sensitive images are also called his image maps.

Image maps can be created in two ways:

- Server-side image maps – The ismap attribute of the image tag enables this. This will require access to related image map processing and server applications.

- Client-side image maps – The usemap attribute of the image tag is used for creating this. This will be used with the corresponding <area> and <map> tags.

Server-side image maps

In the server-side image map, you simply add your image in a hyperlink. After adding the image, we will use the ismap attribute. This attribute will create a special image. Whenever a visitor clicks on that image, coordinates of the mouse pointer will be passed by the browser with the URL. It is the job of the server to decide the document to be sent to the browser based on the mouse pointer coordinates.

Mouse position coordinates are screen pixels that are counted from the image's top left corner. The coordinates start with (0,0). At the end of the URL, these coordinates will be added. A question mark precedes the coordinates.

Example

<!DOCTYPE html>

<html>

<head>

<title>ISMAP Hyperlink Example</title>

</head>

<body>

<p>Click following link</p>

```
<a href="/cgi-bin/ismap.cgi" target="_self">
```

```
  <img ismap src="/images/logo.png" alt="Tutorials Point"
border="0"/>
```

```
</a>
```

```
</body>
```

```
</html>
```

The following search parameters will be sent by the browser to the web server. The web server will then process the characters using the map file or the ismap.cgi. The desired documents can be linked to the coordinates.

/cgi-bin/ismap.cgi?20,30

Using this, several links can be assigned to different coordinates of a given image. By clicking on these coordinates, corresponding links can be opened.

Client-side image maps

You can enable client-side image maps by using the attribute usemap.

The map image will be added to the page using the <img /> tag. An extra attribute usemap will be carried.

Here is a simple example showing client-side image maps.

Example

```
<!DOCTYPE html>
```

```
<html>
```

```
<head>
```

```
<title>USEMAP Hyperlink Example</title>

</head>

<body>

<p>Search and click the hotspot</p>

<img src=/images/html.gif alt="HTML Map" border="0"
usemap="#html"/>

<!-- Create Mappings -->

<map name="html">

 <area shape="circle"

 coords="80,80,20" href="/css/index.htm" alt="CSS Link"
target="_self" />

 <area shape="rect"

 coords="5,5,40,40"               alt="jQuery        Link"
href="/jquery/index.htm" target="_self" />

</map>

</body>

</html>
```

Coordinate system

The value of the coordinates completely depends on the shape
of the item, which can be rectangular or circular. A summary
with detailed examples is given below.

rect = x1 , y1 , x2 , y2

For a rectangle, the upper left corner coordinates are x1 and y1 and the coordinates on the lower right corner are x2 and y2.

circle = xc , yc , radius

The center of a circle is defined by the coordinates xc and yc. The radius of the circle is simply the radius.

Email links

Adding an email link is very easy, but it may result in spam. To avoid spamming, you can implement a different method where you allow users to fill in forms and then use a CGI or PHP script to send them emails.

The default email body and default email subject can be specified alongside your email address. Here is an example in which the default body and subject are used.

Example

```
<a
href="mailto:abc@example.com?subject=Feedback&body=Message">
```

Send Feedback

```
</a>
```

The above code will generate a link and you can use it for sending emails.

Chapter 11:
Frames & iFrames

Frames

Your browser window can be divided into multiple sections using HTML frames. A separate HTML document can be loaded in each of these sections. A frameset is the collection of frames in a given browser window. The division of a window into frames is similar to the organization of rows and columns in a table.

However, using frames has a number of drawbacks, and it is not recommended to use them in most webpages.

- Not all devices can cope with frames. Those with smaller screens often cannot divide the window into different frames.

- The webpage will be displayed in different ways on different computers, based on their screen resolution.

- The back button on the browser might not work in the usual way.

- Some browsers cannot display frames at all.

Creating frames

For frames, you use the **<frameset>** tag in place of the <body> tag. The <frameset> tag is used for defining how windows are divided into frames. The horizontal frames and the vertical frames are defined by the rows and cols attributes respectively. The **<frame>** tag is used for indicating different windows and the HTML documents that are to be opened in the frame. The below example creates three horizontal frames.

Example

```
<!DOCTYPE html>
<html>
<head>
<title>HTML Frames</title>
</head>
<frameset rows="10%,80%,10%">
  <frame name="top" src="/html/top_frame.htm" />
  <frame name="main" src="/html/main_frame.htm" />
  <frame name="bottom" src="/html/bottom_frame.htm" />
  <noframes>
  <body>
    Your browser does not support frames.
  </body>
  </noframes>
</frameset>
</html>
```

Here, we will use the above example but will replace the rows attribute with the cols attribute. We will also change the width, creating three vertical frames.

Example

```
<!DOCTYPE html>
<html>
<head>
<title>HTML Frames</title>
</head>
<frameset cols="25%,50%,25%">
  <frame name="left" src="/html/top_frame.htm" />
  <frame name="center" src="/html/main_frame.htm" />
  <frame name="right" src="/html/bottom_frame.htm" />
  <noframes>
  <body>
    Your browser does not support frames.
  </body>
  </noframes>
</frameset>
</html>
```

The <frame> tag attributes

Some of the important <frame> tag attributes are given below.

Attribute	Description
src	The src attitude is used for giving the filename to be loaded in the frame. Its value can be any URL. For example, giving the src as "/html/top_frame.htm" will simply load the HTML file from the html directory.
Name	You can use this attribute to name the frame. In this way the document to be loaded in a frame can be indicated. This can be used in cases where you want to create links in a frame which load pages in a different frame. In this case, the latter will need a name so it can be identified as the links' target.
Frameborder	This attribute is used to specify whether the borders of the given frame are shown. The given value in the frameborder attribute will be overridden. It will be overridden on the <frameset> tag if one is given. It can take the values of zero and one only. Zero means no and one means yes.

Marginwidth	Using this attribute, the width of the gap between the right and left frame content and frame borders can be specified. The width will be given in pixels.
Marginheight	This attribute can be used to specify the height of the gap between the top and bottom frame content and frame borders. The height will be given in pixels.
Noresize	By default, users can click and drag on the frame borders to resize the frame. You can prevent users from resizing the frame by using the noresize attribute.
Scrolling	The scrollbar appearance on the frame can be controlled using this attribute. It can take the value of "auto", "yes" or "no".
longdesc	Using this attribute, you can add a link that redirects the user to a different page which has a long description on the frame contents. e.g: longdesc="framedescription.htm"

Browser support for frames

If the user's browser doesn't support frames, as when the user has an obsolete browser, the user should be shown the <noframes> element.

As the <body> element will be replaced by the <frameset> element, the <body> element should be placed inside the <noframes> element. In cases where the <frameset> element cannot be understood by the browser, it will understand the content inside the <body> element that is in turn contained inside the <noframes> element.

A message can be added for users whose browsers do not support frames.

Frame name and target attributes

Adding navigation bars in a frame and separately loading the main pages is the most popular use for frames. Here is a simple example.

Example

```
<!DOCTYPE html>

<html>

<head>

<title>HTML Target Frames</title>

</head>

<frameset cols="200, *">

  <frame src="/html/menu.htm" name="menu_page" />
```

```
<frame src="/html/main.htm" name="main_page" />

<noframes>

<body>

    Your browser does not support frames.

</body>

</noframes>

</frameset>

</html>
```

Here, two columns were created and two frames will be added in them. The first frame has a width of 200 pixels and has the navigation menu bar in it. The menu.htm file is used to implement the navigation menu bar. The remaining space will be filled by the second column. The main part of the page is present in the second column. The main.htm file is used for implementing the main part of the page. There are three links present on the menu bar, and main_page is mentioned as the target frame. If any of the links on the menu bar are clicked, main_page will be opened by the available link.

Example

menu.htm contents:

```
<!DOCTYPE html>

<html>

<body bgcolor="#4a7d49">

<a                               href="http://www.google.com"
target="main_page">Google</a>
```


<a   href="http://www.microsoft.com"
target="main_page">Microsoft</a>

<a   href="http://news.bbc.co.uk"   target="main_page">BBC
News</a>

</body>

</html>

main.htm contents:

<!DOCTYPE html>

<html>

<body bgcolor="#b5dcb3">

<h3>This is main page and content from any link will be
displayed here.</h3>

<p>So now click any link and see the result.</p>

</body>

</html>

The output will be produced when the test.htm file is loaded.

The possible values of the target attribute are given below:

Option	Description
_self	The page will be loaded in the current

	frame.
_blank	A new window will be opened and the page will be loaded in the new window.
_parent	The page will be loaded in the parent window. This will only happen in case of a single frameset.
_top	The current frame will be replaced by loading the page in the browser window.
Targetframe	The page will be loaded in the named targetframe.

iframes

An in-line frame can be defined using the HTML tag **<iframe>**. The <iframe> tag is not related to <frameset>. It can be placed anywhere in the document. A rectangular region will be defined within the document by the <iframe> tag, which the browser can show as a separate document. It can even have its own borders and scroll bars.

For specifying the URL, the src attribute can be used. The following example will help you get a better understanding of how to use iframes.

Example

```
<!DOCTYPE html>

<html>

<head>

<title>HTML Iframes</title>

</head>

<body>

<p>Document content goes here...</p>

<iframe src="/html/menu.htm" width="555" height="200">

  Sorry your browser does not support inline frames.

</iframe>

<p>Document content also go here...</p>

</body>

</html>
```

The above code will produce the following output

Document content goes here...

Document content can also go here...

Chapter 12:
Blocks

All of the elements in HTML can be categorized as either block level elements or inline elements.

Block elements

On the screen, block elements appear as if they are preceded and followed by a line break. Examples of block elements are <p>, <h1>, <h2>, <h3>, <h4>, <h5>, <h6>, <ul>, <ol>, <dl>, <pre>, <hr />, <blockquote>, and <address>. All of these elements start on a new line and the content following these elements will also appear on a new line.

Inline elements

Unlike block elements, inline elements can be placed inside sentences; they need not be placed on a new line. Examples of inline elements are <b>, <i>, <u>, <em>, <strong>, <sup>, <sub>, <big>, <small>, <li>, <ins>, <del>, <code>, <cite>, <dfn>, <kbd>, and <var>.

Grouping HTML elements

There are two very frequently used tags for grouping different HTML tags. They are the **<div>** tag and the **<span>** tag.

The <div> tag

The <div> tag is an important block level tag which is used for grouping other HTML tags. It is also used for applying cascading style sheets on a given group of elements. Though it doesn't provide a visual change on a given block, it becomes significant when used with cascading style sheets.

Example

```
<!DOCTYPE html>

<html>

<head>

<title>HTML div Tag</title>

</head>

<body>

<!-- First group of tags -->

<div style="color:red">

  <h4>This is first group</h4>

  <p>Following is a list of cars</p>

  <ul>

  <li>BMW</li>

  <li>Nissan</li>

  <li>Jaguar</li>

  <li>Mercedes</li>

  </ul>

</div>

  <!-- Second group of tags -->
```

```
<div style="color:green">
 <h4>This is second group</h4>
 <p>Following is a list of bikes</p>
 <ul>
 <li>Aprilia</li>
 <li>KTM</li>
 <li>Ducati</li>
 <li>Honda</li>
 </ul>
</div>
</body>
</html>
```

The above code will produce the following output.

THIS IS FIRST GROUP

Following is a list of cars

- BMW

- Nissan

- Jaguar

- Mercedes

THIS IS SECOND GROUP

Following is a list of bikes

- Aprilia

- KTM

- Ducati

- Honda

The <span> tag

For grouping inline elements in a given HTML document, we will use the HTML <span> tag. Like the <div> tag, it doesn't provide a visual change on a given block, but becomes significant when used with cascading style sheets.

The main difference between the <div> tag and the <span> tag is that they are used for grouping block elements and inline elements respectively.

Example

<!DOCTYPE html>

<html>

<head>

<title>HTML span Tag</title>

</head>

<body>

<p>This is <span style="color:red">red</span> and this is <span style="color:green">green</span></p>

</body>

</html>

The above code will produce an output with red and green colored text.

Chapter 13:
Background

The default background for all webpages is white, but this can be changed. You can add either images or colors to your background to decorate your webpage. Here, we will look at these methods one at a time.

HTML background with colors

To change the background you can use the bgcolor attribute. The syntax for using the bgcolor attribute is given below:

<tagname bgcolor="color_value"...>

You can change this color_value by using any of the following formats:

<!-- Format 1 - Use color name -->

<table bgcolor="lime" >

<!-- Format 2 - Use hex value -->

<table bgcolor="#f1f1f1" >

<!-- Format 3 - Use color value in RGB terms -->

<table bgcolor="rgb(0,0,120)" >

Here are a few examples in which the background is set.

Example

<!DOCTYPE html>

<html>

```html
<head>
<title>HTML Background Colors</title>
</head>
<body>
<!-- Format 1 - Use color name -->
<table bgcolor="yellow" width="100%">
<tr><td>
This background is yellow
</td></tr>
</table>
<!-- Format 2 - Use hex value -->
<table bgcolor="#6666FF" width="100%">
<tr><td>
This background is sky blue
</td></tr>
</table>
<!-- Format 3 - Use color value in RGB terms -->
<table bgcolor="rgb(255,0,255)" width="100%">
<tr><td>
This background is green
</td></tr>
```

```
</table>

</body>

</html>
```

This code will give us the following output:

This background is yellow

This background is sky blue

This background is green

Patterned & transparent backgrounds

You may have seen webpages with transparent or patterned backgrounds. Using backgrounds will enhance the look of your webpage, increase readability and grab attention. Try to choose the correct background for your webpage. Using simpler backgrounds with colors matching the font is recommended.

To avoid slow loading, it is advised that you use images, including transparent GIF and PNG images, with the smallest available resolution. In this example we will set the background pattern for a table.

Example

```
<!DOCTYPE html>

<html>

<head>

<title>HTML Background Images</title>

</head>
```

```html
<body>

<!-- Set a table background using pattern -->

<table background="/images/pattern1.gif" width="100%" height="100">

<tr><td>

This background is filled up with a pattern image.

</td></tr>

</table>

<!-- Another example on table background using pattern -->

<table background="/images/pattern2.gif" width="100%" height="100">

<tr><td>

This background is filled up with a pattern image.

</td></tr>

</table>

</body>

</html>
```

This code will give output with a background with the selected patterns.

Chapter 14:
Fonts

Fonts are very important in making a webpage user-friendly and the increasing readability. The color and typeface of the font will entirely depend on the browser and the computer on which the webpage is displayed. For adding font color, size and style, we use the **<font>** tag. For setting the same color, typeface and size to all the text on the webpage you can use the **<basefont>** tag.

There are three attributes – the size, color and face attributes – that allow you to customize your fonts. With the <font> tag, one or all of the font attributes of your webpage can be changed at any given time. Remember that if you don't use a closing tag, the text following the starting tag will be changed to the end.

Set font size

You can use the size attribute to set the font size for your content. This attribute accepts values from 1 to 7. The default value for the size attribute is 3.

Example

<!DOCTYPE html>

<html>

<head>

<title>Setting Font Size</title>

</head>

```
<body>
<font size="1">Font size="1"</font><br />
<font size="2">Font size="2"</font><br />
<font size="3">Font size="3"</font><br />
<font size="4">Font size="4"</font><br />
<font size="5">Font size="5"</font><br />
<font size="6">Font size="6"</font><br />
<font size="7">Font size="7"</font>
</body>
</html>
```

This code will produce the following output:

Font size="1"

Font size="2"

Font size="3"

Font size="4"

Font size="5"

Font size="6"

Font size="7"

Here is an example of relative font size.

Example

```
<!DOCTYPE html>
<html>
<head>
<title>Relative Font Size</title>
</head>
<body>
<font size="-1">Font size="-1"</font><br />
<font size="+1">Font size="+1"</font><br />
<font size="+2">Font size="+2"</font><br />
<font size="+3">Font size="+3"</font><br />
<font size="+4">Font size="+4"</font>
</body>
</html>
```

This will produce following result:

Font size="-1"

Font size="+1"

Font size="+2"

Font size="+3"

Font size="+4"

Chapter 15:
Forms

In some situations you will want to collect data from visitors. You can use HTML forms do to this. For instance, you may need to collect information like credit card numbers and postal addresses from customers.

A HTML form collects information from the user and sends it to backend applications like ASP, CGI or PHP script. The passed data will be processed by the backend application according to the business logic defined inside the application.

There are a number of formal elements available, such as text area fields, text fields, check boxes, radio buttons and dropdown menus.

To create forms, we use the HTML **<form>** tag. The syntax for creating a HTML form is given below:

<form action="Script URL" method="GET|POST">

  form elements like input, text area etc.

</form>

Form attributes

Here is a list of the most widely used attributes apart from the common form attributes.

Attribute	Description
action	This is the backend script that is ready to process the data that you have passed.
method	This attribute is used for uploading the data. The GET and POST methods are the most frequently used methods.
target	This attribute can be used to specify the target frame or target window. The script result will be displayed in them. Values like _self, _blank, _blank etc, will be taken.
enctype	This attribute is used to specify the method by which your browser encodes the data. Your browser will encode the data before sending it. The possible values are given below. • **application/x-www-form-urlencoded** – This is used in most simple scenarios and it is a standard method for most of the forms. • **mutlipart/form-data** – You can use this in cases where you upload binary data. This binary data can be in the form of a Word file, images etc.

HTML form controls

There are many form controls that can be used to collect data. They include:

- Text Input Controls

- Radio Box Controls

- Clickable Buttons

- Submit and Reset Button

- File Select boxes

- Hidden Controls

- Checkboxes Controls

- Select Box Controls

Text input controls

There are a total of three text input controls for forms:

- Single-line text input controls – Not all items need multiple input lines from the user. In fact, most inputs require only a single line, such as search boxes, user ID boxes etc. The **<input>** tag is used for creating single text line input controls.

- Password input controls – Like single line text input controls, password input controls are also single line. The password input control will immediately mask the character when the user enters it. Password input controls are created with the HTML **<input>** tag.

- Multiline text input controls −Multiline text input controls are provided in situations where the user is required to submit details longer than a single line. The HTML **<textarea>** tag is used for creating multiline input controls.

Single-line text input controls

The single line text input control can be used for items that don't require more than one line of input from the user, such as search boxes and names. The HTML <input> tag is used for creating single-line text input controls. Here is a simple example where the single line text input is used for taking the first and last names of the user.

Example

<!DOCTYPE html>

<html>

<head>

<title>Text Input Control</title>

</head>

<body>

<form >

First name: <input type="text" name="first_name" />

Last name: <input type="text" name="last_name" />

</form>

144

```
</body>

</html>
```

The above code will produce an output where the first name and last name of the user are requested.

First name:

Last name:

The following table shows the list of attributes for the <input> tag for creating a text field:

Attribute	Description
type	The type of input control can be indicated for the text input control. The attribute will be set to **text**.
name	The name of the control can be given with this attribute. This name will be later sent to the server. The server will recognize it and then get the value.
value	Inside the control, this attribute can be used to specify the initial value.
size	Using this attribute, the text input control width can be specified. This width will be given in terms of characters.

maxlength	The maximum number of characters which the user can enter can be specified using this attribute.

Password input controls

Though this is a single line text input, the characters will be masked as the user enters them. These are also created using the input tag, but the attribute is **password**. Here is a simple example of the single line password input used for taking a user's password.

Example

```
<!DOCTYPE html>

<html>

<head>

<title>Password Input Control</title>

</head>

<body>

<form >

User ID :  <input type="text" name="user_id" />

<br>

Password:  <input type="password" name="password" />

</form>

</body>
```

</html>

The attributes for creating a password field are listed in the table below:

Attribute	Description
type	This attribute is used to indicate the input control type; for passwords, it will be set to **password**.
name	This attribute will give a name to the control and this name will later be sent to the server. The server will recognize the value and retrieve it.
value	This attribute can be used to provide an initial value.
size	The width of the text input control can be specified using this attribute. It will be in terms of characters.
maxlength	The maximum number of characters can be specified using this attribute. Characters over the maximum number cannot be entered.

Multiline text input controls

Sometimes users may need to provide information that is more than a single sentence in length. Using the HTML <textarea> tag, you can create multiline input controls. In this example, the multiline text input is used for taking an item description.

Example

<!DOCTYPE html>

<html>

<head>

<title>Multiple-Line Input Control</title>

</head>

<body>

<form>

Description :

<textarea rows="5" cols="50" name="description">

Enter description here...

</textarea>

</form>

</body>

</html>

The following table shows the list of attributes for the <textarea> tag:

Attribute	Description
name	Used to give a name to the control which is sent to the server for recognition and retrieval of the value.
rows	Indicates the number of rows of the text area box.
cols	Indicates the number of columns of the text area box

Checkbox Control

In some situations users will have to select more than one option. In such cases, you can use checkboxes. Checkboxes can be created using the HTML <input> tag. The attribute type should be set to checkbox. Here is a simple HTML code for a form with checkboxes.

Example

<!DOCTYPE html>

<html>

<head>

<title>Checkbox Control</title>

</head>

```
<body>

<form>

<input type="checkbox" name="Turbo" value="on"> Turbo

<input type="checkbox" name="Super Charged" value="on">
Super Charged

</form>

</body>

</html>
```

The above code will produce the following output.

Turbo Super Charged

The attributes of the checkbox tag are given below:

Attribute	Description
type	This attribute is used for indicating the input control type. The input control type for checkbox should be set to **checkbox.**
name	This attribute gives the control a name. This name will later be sent to the server and the server will get the value after recognizing it.
value	The checkbox value will be selected.
checked	For it to be selected by default, set it to

checked.

Radio button control

There will be situations where you will have to select one option out of many. Radio buttons are used in such situations. Radio buttons can be created with the <input> tag, but type attribute is set to radio. Here is a simple HTML code which has a form with two radio buttons.

Example

<!DOCTYPE html>

<html>

<head>

<title>Radio Box Control</title>

</head>

<body>

<form>

<input type="radio" name="subject" value="Turbo"> Turbo

<input type="radio" name="subject" value="Super Charged"> Super Charged

</form>

</body>

</html>

151

The above code will produce the following output.

Turbo Super Charged

The radio button attributes are given below:

Attribute	Description
type	This attribute is used for indicating the input control type; for the radio button input control, it will be **radio.**
name	This attribute is used to give a name that will be later sent to the server. The server will get a value after recognizing it.
value	Use this attribute to select the radio works value.
checked	If you wish to select it by default, you should set it to checked.

Select box control

Sometimes you should allow the user to select an option from a list. In such cases you can use the select box. The select box is also called the dropdown box. A dropdown box will show a list of items and the user can select any of those. Here is a simple HTML code with a form having a single drop down box.

Example

```
<!DOCTYPE html>
<html>
<head>
<title>Select Box Control</title>
</head>
<body>
<form>
<select name="dropdown">
<option value="Turbo" selected>Turbo</option>
<option value="SuperCharged">SuperCharged</option>
</select>
</form>
</body>
</html>
```

This will produce following result:

Turbo SuperCharged

The following is a list of important attributes of the **<select>**
tag:

Attribute	Description
name	This attribute is used to give your control a name. This name will be later sent to the server and the server will recognize it. After recognizing it, the server will send a value.
size	This is used to present a scrolling list box.
multiple	If this attribute is set to multiple, users will be allowed to select more than one item from the list.

Important **<option>** tag attributes are given below:

Attribute	Description
value	The value that will be used if an option in the select box is selected.
selected	Specifies that this option should be the initially selected value when the page loads.
label	An alternative way of labeling options

File upload box

You will sometimes want to let the user upload a file to your website. In such cases, you should use the file upload box, which is also known as the file select box. This can be created using the <input> tag. The attribute should be set as **file**.

Example

<!DOCTYPE html>

<html>

<head>

<title>File Upload Box</title>

</head>

<body>

<form>

<input type="file" name="fileupload" accept="image/*" />

</form>

</body>

</html>

The important file upload box attributes are given below:

Attribute	Description
name	This is used for giving your name to the control. It is then sent to the server, which will

	recognize it and send the value.
accept	This is used to specify the file types that the server accepts.

Button controls

In HTML, clickable buttons can be created in a number of ways. A clickable button can be created using the <input> tag. This can be done by setting **button** as its type attribute. The following values can be given to this type attribute:

Type	Description
submit	This will create a button which submits a form automatically.
reset	This will create a button which resets the form controls automatically to its initial values.
button	This is used for creating a button which triggers the client-side script.
image	This is used for creating a clickable button as the background. An image can be used.

Here is an example in which a form with three different buttons is displayed.

Example

```
<!DOCTYPE html>

<html>

<head>

<title>File Upload Box</title>

</head>

<body>

<form>

<input type="submit" name="submit" value="Submit" />

<input type="reset" name="reset" value="Reset" />

<input type="button" name="ok" value="OK" />

<input          type="image"          name="imagebutton"
src="/html/images/logo.png" />

</form>

</body>

</html>
```

This code will produce an output displaying three form buttons.

Hidden form controls

Data can be hidden inside the webpage by using the hidden form controls. This hidden data can be later pushed to the server. This control will not be displayed on the webpage but will be hidden inside the code. Here is an example where a hidden form is used for keeping the page number of the current page. The hidden control value will be sent to the server whenever the user clicks on the next page. The server will decide the next page to be displayed based on the current page.

Example

<!DOCTYPE html>

<html>

<head>

<title>File Upload Box</title>

</head>

<body>

<form>

<p>This is page 10</p>

<input type="hidden" name="pagename" value="10" />

<input type="submit" name="submit" value="Submit" />

<input type="reset" name="reset" value="Reset" />

</form>

</body>

```
</html>
```

The above code will produce the following output:

This is page 10

Chapter 16: Marquees

Plain text can be boring, and it doesn't really grab the attention of webpage visitors. Now imagine seeing scrolling text on the webpage. This immediately grabs attention and makes the webpage interesting. Important text or images can be placed in between the marquee tags to make them scroll on your webpage.

In HTML, marquee is scrolling text. This text can scroll horizontally or vertically on your webpage depending on the settings used. We use the **<marquee>** tag to make the text scroll. This is not supported by all browsers, and in such cases you can use the tags from JavaScript or CSS to get a similar effect. The syntax for the HTML <marquee> tag is given below:

<marquee   attribute_name="attribute_value"....more attributes>

Any content can be placed in between these tags.

</marquee>

Some of the important attributes that can be used with the <marquee> tag are given in the following table:

Attribute	Description
Width	This attribute is used to specify the width of the marquee. This attribute can take values like 10 or 20% etc.

Height	This attribute is used to specify the height of the marquee. This attribute can take values like 10 or 20% etc.
Direction	This attribute is used to specify the direction of the marquee. This attribute can take the values right, left, up or down.
Behavior	This attribute is used to specify the scrolling of the marquee. This attribute can take the values scroll, alternate or slide.
scrolldelay	This attribute is used to specify the time delay between each jump. This attribute can take values like 10 etc.
scrollamount	This attribute is used to specify the speed with which the marquee text scrolls.
Loop	This attribute is used to specify the number of times to loop. The default value for this attribute is INFINITE, meaning that the marquee will continue to loop endlessly.
Bgcolor	This attribute is used to specify the background color in the items. These colors can be given in terms of color hex value or color names.
Hspace	This attribute is used to specify the marquee's

	horizontal space. This can take values like 10, 15 or 20% etc.
Vspace	This attribute is used to specify the marquee's vertical space. This can take values like 10, 15 or 20% etc.

Here are a few examples that demonstrate the use of these tags:

Example 1

```
<!DOCTYPE html>

<html>

<head>

<title>HTML marquee Tag</title>

</head>

<body>

<marquee>This is basic example of marquee</marquee>

</body>

</html>
```

This code will give the following output:

This is basic example of marquee

Example 2

```
<!DOCTYPE html>

<html>

<head>

<title>HTML marquee Tag</title>

</head>

<body>

<marquee width="50%">This example will take only 50% width</marquee>

</body>

</html>
```

This code will give the following output:

This example will take only 50% width

Example 3

```
<!DOCTYPE html>

<html>

<head>

<title>HTML marquee Tag</title>

</head>

<body>

<marquee direction="right">This text will scroll from left to right</marquee>
```

```html
</body>
</html>
```

This code will give the following output:

This text will scroll from left to right

Example 4

```html
<!DOCTYPE html>
<html>
<head>
<title>HTML marquee Tag</title>
</head>
<body>
<marquee direction="up">This text will scroll from bottom to top</marquee>
</body>
</html>
```

This code will give the following output:

This text will scroll from bottom to top

Example 5

```html
<!DOCTYPE html>
<html>
<head>
```

```
<title>HTML marquee Tag</title>

</head>

<body>

<marquee behavior="scroll" direction="left"
scrollamount="1">Slow scroll speed</marquee>

</body>

</html>
```

Example 6

```
<!DOCTYPE html>

<html>

<head>

<title>HTML marquee Tag</title>

</head>

<body>

<marquee behavior="scroll" direction="left"
scrollamount="10">Medium scroll speed</marquee>

</body>

</html>
```

Example 7

```
<!DOCTYPE html>

<html>

<head>
```

```html
<title>HTML marquee Tag</title>

</head>

<body>

<marquee behavior="scroll" direction="left" scrollamount="20">Fast scroll speed</marquee>

</body>

</html>
```

Example 8

```html
<!DOCTYPE html>

<html>

<head>

<title>HTML marquee Tag</title>

</head>

<body>

<marquee behavior="scroll" direction="left"><img src="/pix/smile.gif" width="100" height="100" alt="smile" /></marquee>speed</marquee>

</body>

</html>
```

This code will add an image that scrolls from right to left.

Example 9

```
<!DOCTYPE html>

<html>

<head>

<title>HTML marquee Tag</title>

</head>

<body>

<marquee behavior="scroll" direction="left">

<img src="/pix/smile.gif" width="100" height="100" alt="smile" />

<p>Sample text under a <a href="/html/codes/scrolling_images.cfm">scrolling image</a>.</p>

</marquee>

</body>

</html>
```

This code will make both the image and text to scroll from right to left.

Example 10

```
<!DOCTYPE html>

<html>

<head>

<title>HTML marquee Tag</title>
```

```
</head>

<body>

<marquee behavior="alternate">Your bouncing text goes
here</marquee>

</body>

</html>
```

This code will display text that bounces between the sides.

Chapter 17:
Cascading Style Sheets (CSS)

CSS, or Cascading Style Sheets, are used for describing how HTML documents are presented or pronounced. Since the foundation of the consortium in 1994, the W3C has actively promoted the usage of style sheets.

Cascading Style Sheets provide easy and effective alternatives to specify various attributes for HTML tags. Using CSS, you can specify a number of style properties for a given HTML element. Each property has a name and a value, separated by a colon (:). Each property declaration is separated by a semi-colon (;).

Here we will consider an example in which the <font> tag and its color and size attributes are used.

Example

```
<!DOCTYPE html>

<html>

<head>

<title>HTML CSS</title>

</head>

<body>

<p><font color="green" size="5">Hello, World!</font></p>

</body>

</html>
```

The above example can be rewritten using CSS as below:

```
<!DOCTYPE html>
<html>
<head>
<title>HTML CSS</title>
</head>
<body>
<p style="color:green;font-size:24px;">Hello, World!</p>
</body>
</html>
```

The above example will give us the following output:

Hello, World!

Uses of CSS in HTML

In HTML, CSS can be used in three different ways:

- External Style Sheet – This is for defining style sheet rules in a separate file. This file can be included a HTML document with the <link> tag.

- Internal Style Sheet – Here, we'll define the style sheet rules inside the HTML document's header section using the <style> tag.

- Inline Style Sheet – Here, the style sheet rules will be defined alongside the HTML elements. These style sheets will be defined using the **style** attribute.

Now we will look at each of these three cases with examples.

External style sheet

If you're planning to use a particular timesheet for multiple pages, it is recommended that you define a style sheet common to all of the pages in a separate file. The cascading style sheet file has the .css extension and is included inside the HTML files using the <link> tag.

Example

Here, we will define a style sheet with the name style.css that has the given rules:

.red{

  color: red;

}

.thick{

  font-size:20px;

}

.green{

  color:green;

}

We have defined three rules in CSS that will be applied to three different classes. Now, we will use this external CSS file in our HTML document.

```html
<!DOCTYPE html>
<html>
<head>
<title>HTML External CSS</title>
<link rel="stylesheet" type="text/css" href="/html/style.css">
</head>
<body>
<p class="red">This text looks red</p>
<p class="thick">This text is thick</p>
<p class="green">This text looks green</p>
<p class="thick green">This is both green and thick</p>
</body>
</html>
```

This example will give us the following output:

This text looks red

This text is thick

This text looks green

This is both green and thick

Internal style sheet

In some situations, you will need to apply style sheet rules to a single document and that document alone. In such cases, the rules can be included inside the header section of the HTML document. This can be done by using the <style> tag.

If there are rules defined outside the external CSS file, the rules that are defined inside the style sheet will override them. Let's consider the above example again. Now, we will rewrite the HTML code with the rules inside the HTML document using the <style> tag.

Example

```
<!DOCTYPE html>

<html>

<head>

<title>HTML Internal CSS</title>

<style type="text/css">

.red{

  color: red;

}

.thick{

  font-size:20px;

}

.green{

  color:green;

}

</style>
```

```
</head>

<body>

<p class="red">This text looks red</p>

<p class="thick">This text is thick</p>

<p class="green">This text looks green</p>

<p class="thick green">This is both green and thick</p>

</body>

</html>
```

This will display the following output:

This text looks red

This text is thick

This text looks green

This is both green and thick

Inline style sheet

By using the style attribute of the relevant tag, the style sheet rules can be directly applied to HTML elements. This should only be done if you want to make a particular kind of change in a given HTML element.

The rules that are defined within the element will override the rules that are defined outside in an external CSS file. Now we will rewrite the examples given above, this time using the style attribute for writing style sheet rules.

Example

```
<!DOCTYPE html>
<html>
<head>
<title>HTML Inline CSS</title>
</head>
<body>
<p style="color:red;">This text looks red</p>
<p style="font-size:20px;">This text is thick</p>
<p style="color:green;">This text looks green</p>
<p style="color:green;font-size:20px;">This is both green and thick</p>
</body>
</html>
```

This will display the following output:

This text looks red

This text is thick

This text looks green

This is both green and thick

Chapter 18:
HTML Reference Tags

The reference tags in HTML and their descriptions are given below:

Tag	Description
<!--...-->	This tag is used to specify a comment.
<!DOCTYPE>	This tag is used to specify the document type.
<a>	This tag is used to specify an anchor.
<abbr>	This tag is used to specify an abbreviation.
<acronym>	This tag is used to specify an acronym.
<address>	This tag is used to specify an address element.
<applet>	This tag is used to specify an applet.
<area>	This tag is used to specify a particular area in an image map.

<u>**<article>**</u>	This tag is used to specify an article
<aside>	This tag is used to specify some content that loosely related to the page content. Even if this content is deleted, the remaining content will still make sense.
<audio>	Sound content can be specified with this tag
<b>	Bold text can be specified with this tag.
<u>**<base>**</u>	A base URL can be specified with this tag.
<u>**<basefont>**</u>	A base font can be specified using this tag.
<u>**<bdo>**</u>	The text display direction will be specified with this tag.
<u>**<bgsound>**</u>	The background music can be specified with this tag.
<u>**<big>**</u>	Big text can be specified with this tag.
<u>**<blink>**</u>	Blinking text will be specified with this

	tag.
<blockquote>	Long quotation will be specified with this tag.
<body>	The element of the body will be specified by this tag.
** **	A single line break will be inserted by this tag.
<button>	The pushbutton will be specified with this tag.
<canvas>	Using this tag, graphics can be made with a script.
<caption>	A table caption will be specified with this tag.
<center>	Centered text will be specified by this tag.
<cite>	This will specify a citation.
<code>	The computer code text can be specified with this tag.

<col>	The table column attributes can be specified with this tag.
<colgroup>	A group of table columns can be specified using this tag.
<comment>	This will put a comment within the document.
<datalist>	This tag is used to specify the list of input options.
<dd>	A definition description can be specified using this tag.
<del>	Deleted text can be specified using this tag.
<dfn>	Definition terms can be specified using this tag.
<dialog>	A window or dialogue box can be specified with this tag.
<dir>	A directory list will be specified with this tag.

<div>	A section in the document can be specified using this tag.
<dl>	A definition list can be specified using this tag.
<dt>	A definition term can be specified using this tag.
<em>	Emphasized text can be specified using this tag.
<embed>	An external application container can be specified using this tag.
<fieldset>	Fieldset can be specified with this tag.
<figcaption>	The figure element caption can be specified with this tag.
<figure>	Self-contained content can be specified with this tag.
<font>	The text font, color and size can be specified with this tag.
<footer>	The footer of a section or document can

	be specified using this tag.
<form>	A form can be specified using this tag.
<frame>	A sub window can be specified using this tag.
<frameset>	A set of frames can be specified with this tag.
<h1> to <h6>	Headers 1 to 6 can be specified with this tag.
<head>	The document's information can be specified by this tag.
<header>	The header for a section or a document can be specified by this tag.
<hr>	A horizontal rule can be specified with this tag.
<html>	A HTML document can be specified with this tag.
<i>	The italic text can be specified using this tag.

\<iframe\>	An inline window frame can be specified using this tag.
\<ilayer\>	An in-line layer can be specified using this tag.
\<img\>	Images can be specified using this tag.
\<input\>	Input field can be specified using this tag.
\<ins\>	Inserted text can be specified.
\<isindex\>	A single line input field can be specified.
\<kbd\>	Keyboard text can be specified using this tag.
\<keygen\>	The key information can be generated in the form using this tag.
\<label\>	A form control label can be specified using this tag.
\<layer\>	A layer can be specified using this tag.
\<legend\>	Fieldset title can be specified with this

	tag.
<li>	A list item can be specified with this tag.
<link>	A resources reference can be specified using this tag.
<main>	Specifies the main or important content in the document, if there is only one element in the document.
<map>	This tag can be used to specify an image map.
<mark>	The highlighted text can be specified for reference purposes.
<marquee>	This tag can create a marquee.
<menu>	A menu list can be specified with this tag.
<menuitem>	The menu or command items that can be invoked by the user from the pop-up menu can be specified.
<meta>	The meta data of the HTML document (which is not shown) can be specified

	using this tag.
<meter>	This tag is used to specify a scalar measurement.
<multicol>	Multi column text flow can be specified using this tag.
<nav>	This tag is used to specify the section containing navigation links.
<nobr>	Breaks will not be allowed inside the enclosed text.
<noembed>	Specifies content to be presented by browsers that do not support the <embed> tag.
<noframes>	A non-frame section can be specified using this tag.
<noscript>	A non-script section can be specified.
<object>	An embedded object can be specified using this tag.
<ol>	An ordered list can be specified using

	this tag.
\<optgroup\>	An option group can be specified using this tag.
\<option\>	The options on the dropdown list can be specified.
\<output\>	The calculation result can be specified with this tag.
\<p\>	Paragraph can be specified using this tag.
\<param\>	An object's parameter can be specified using this tag.
\<plaintext\>	This tag is used for rendering the remaining document as plain text (preformatted).
\<pre\>	This tag can be used to specify preformatted text.
\<progress\>	The completion progress of a given task can be specified using this tag.

<q>	A short quotation can be specified using this tag.
<rt>	A text Ruby annotation can be specified using this tag.
<ruby>	Ruby annotation can be specified using this tag.
<s>	Strikethrough text can be specified using this tag.
<samp>	This tag can be used to specify the sample computer code.
<script>	This tag can be used to specify a script.
<section>	This can be used to specify a section in a document.
<select>	A selectable table can be specified with this tag.
<spacer>	Whitespace can be specified with this tag.
<small>	Small text can be specified with this tag.

<source>	Specifies a media resource for media elements, defined inside video or audio elements
<span>	A section in a document can be specified with this tag.
<strike>	Strikethrough text can be specified with this tag.
<strong>	Strong text can be specified with this tag.
<style>	Style definitions can be specified with this tag.
<sub>	Subscripted text can be specified with this tag.
<summary>	This tag is used to specify a caption, summary or a legend for given <details>.
<sup>	Superscripted text can be specified using this tag.
<table>	A table can be specified with this tag.

<tbody>	A table body can be specified with this tag.
<td>	A table cell can be specified with this tag.
<textarea>	Text area can be specified with this tag.
<tfoot>	A table footer can be specified with this tag.
<th>	A table heading can be specified with this tag.
<thead>	Table headed can be specified with this tag.
<time>	This is used to specify a date and time.
<title>	This is used to specify the document title.
<tr>	This tag is used to specify a row in a table.
<track>	In media players, this is used to specify text tracks.

<tt>	This can be used to specify teletype text.
<u>	This tag is be used to specify underlined text.
<ul>	This tag is used to specify an unordered list.
<var>	Variables can be specified using this tag.
<video>	In media players, video tracks can be specified using this tag.
<wbr>	A potential word breakpoint inside the <nobr> section can be indicated by this tag.
<xmp>	This tag is used to specify preformatted text.

Conclusion

Webpage design sometimes seems wreathed in mysticism and cyber mumbo jumbo, but I hope I've shown you that it's not as scary as you might think. In fact, HTML is actually fairly straightforward. If you're looking for a straightforward hobby that can really accomplish things, then you've come to the right place. These are the foundations upon which you can build your webpages and push on to greater things like CSS, Java, JavaScript, C++, and so on. Remember that you can never really get in over your head if you master and truly understand what it is that you're working on at the moment.

If something doesn't make sense to you or is confusing, my best suggestion is to open up your TextEdit or Notepad and start working on it. Pull it up in your browser and have a look at what it does to your page. Taking everything step by step will eventually lead you down the path of success. There is never an excuse for jumping ahead without fully understanding what it is that you've already done. Keeping notes is a good idea, as this will help you trace your footsteps.

If you ever find yourself needing to get back to the basics or you just don't remember how to do something simple, come back to this book and have a look at the fundamentals. With everything that I have presented to you in this book, you should be able to understand the beginnings of a webpage, and if you can get the beginning, it's just a matter of taking the next steps one at a time. So good luck – now get out there and make an amazing webpage!

Printed in Great Britain
by Amazon